The Good Parts

poems by

Eric Blanchard

Finishing Line Press
Georgetown, Kentucky

The Good Parts

*For those who have inspired me, encouraged me,
and acted as my muse.*

ACKNOWLEDGMENTS

Grateful acknowledgment is made to the journals and anthologies in which
these poems, some of them in earlier versions, first appeared:

Across the Spectrum 2010-2011 (a contest anthology from the Sinclair
    Community College (Dayton, Ohio) Creative Writing Program): "I
    give myself permission"

Amarillo Bay: "I hate this feeling—"

Borderlands: Texas Poetry Review: "Sweet Tea"

Breadcrumb Scabs: "Chasing Freedom" and "Small Things"

Literary Orphans: "The Meeting Ran Long," "Opening the Mind," "The Good
    Parts," and "God Holds Grudges"

Mock Turtle Zine: "The Little Nun That Could" and "Indiana Memories"

Poems From the Far Hills (an anthology of work by the Wright Library
    Poets, published by Wright Memorial Public Library, Dayton,
    Ohio): "Ars Domestica" (as "Ars Poetica")

Rust + Moth: "The Rain Begins"

The Rusty Nail Magazine: "Everyday Strangers"

Shot Glass Journal: "Kicking and Screaming"

Publisher: Leah Maines
Editor: Christen Kincaid
Cover Art and Design: Eric Blanchard
Author Photo: Eric Blanchard

Printed in the USA on acid-free paper.
Order online: www.finishinglinepress.com
        also available on amazon.com

Author inquiries and mail orders:
Finishing Line Press
P. O. Box 1626
Georgetown, Kentucky 40324
U. S. A.

Table of Contents

i.

Opening the Mind...2

Everyday Strangers...3

Chasing Freedom 4

Sweet Tea 5

The Good Parts..6

God Holds Grudges 7

The Test..8

Indiana Memories 9

Today's Poem...10

ii.

Small Things..12

The Little Nun That Could 13

My Would-Be Wife 14

Ars Domestica...16

I hate this feeling— 17

The Rain Begins..18

The Honeymoon That Was Not......................................19

Missing Pieces...21

Winter Storm 22

iii.

The Meeting Ran Long 24

I give myself permission 25

Not a Squirrel..26

Not Quite Empty 27

Kicking and Screaming..28

Something Else Domestic...29

Head-Cold Apocalypse 30

Cigarette-Smoke Nostalgia..31

Recreational Use..32

i.

Opening the Mind

Now this
is the key to passing
one piece of knowledge
to another person's
mind: Take one
tiny microdot
of truth—one
fact plucked
from emotion—
and place it
on your tongue.
Do not savor it
for long. Do
not swallow.
Share it
with the world
one whisper
at a time.
          And
lightning flashes,
sparks fly across synapses,
and sometimes
there is thunder
in the distance.

Everyday Strangers

I walk the same street every morning,
and every morning, the dogs in one yard
bark at me and my dog, as though
they had never seen us before.

And the pot-bellied pig grunts.
He is as big as the two German Shepherds—
one docile and friendly, the other
always angry.

Then two tiny mutts, constant
in their yap yap yapping, begging
to be stepped on. And Buster, walking beside me,
growls his displeasure once we've passed.

The pig thinks he's a dog. I know;
I've watched him. We are everyday strangers—
our paths habitually crossing, like walking in circles,
like clockwork.

Chasing Freedom

I spoke with a man whose wife had just died.
He rambled to me about fixing his sailboat and how
moving to Arizona would be good for his asthma.
He could buy tribal land there cheap,

but his daughter would not abandon her friends to go with him.
If only he had spoken to his sister sometime—
at least once—in the past thirty years.
She lives with the Navajo near Four Corners,

where the Cherokee are welcome.
The older boys are still in denial, he says.
But he (and his wife) had long accepted her fate.
If only he had spoken to his sister.

*Without a ballast keel, you shouldn't venture far from shore
in rough seas*, his thoughts return to the sloop.
(It was not sudden or unexpected.) If only
he had spoken to his sister in Arizona.

As the hour turns late, his wolf-dog grows restless,
and I am suddenly glad she has a leash made of chain.
Florescent trickster eyes follow wildly
a playful cur across the yard, chasing freedom.

Sweet Tea

The Mexican hibiscus grows
wild and unruly and bright green
before it spurts flowers like blood.
The policeman thought it
was pot, because the leaves
look vicious and the neighbors
were smiling. He got tangled up
in the scent and confusion.
He tried to cut it down,
but he could not repossess it.
It makes sweet tea just the same,
as though it were the weed it is—
wild and unruly and green,
with flowers like blood.

The Good Parts

The dead rabbits seem so sad
as grandpa's knife separates fur
from flesh. We are so glad
to have nourishment packed with protein
and luck. We suck marrow
from the bones.

My brother is partial to the brains,
simmered still in the skull
with what's left of a rich stew.
Grandma stitches the skins together
to make a blanket
for the baby's new bed.

           And I
read to him stories of Br'er Rabbit,
of southern post-war reconstruction,
leaving out the good parts—
the jolly poverty and the zip-
a-dee-doo-dah endings.

God Holds Grudges

The one of us who grew too quickly
makes jokes at the rest of our expense.
He laughs at the empathy we share.
He sees nothing clearly, being blind
since birth, both stubborn and angry
at a god who gave him bulk and brawn
but never listens to the prayers he offers,
asking for sunlight—a hint of color,
asking for what other people have.
And still he dances at the altar
and preaches from a raging pulpit
about the sacrament of life and the need
for obedience, unquestioning faith,
and piety. Then he drinks himself stupid
and slaps the whore who lies beside him
across her ruby-red lips because she says
she loves him and that her unborn child
is his. He does not preach forgiveness.
He does not forgive. *God holds grudges,*
he says. And this is how he worships.
This is how he lives his sorry life.

The Test

You have a physics test tomorrow,
after the Sun has rotated around the flat Earth,
chasing a moon made of cheese.

      And God
has placed pinholes in the heavens
for men to marvel about.

He has poked stars
into curtains.

In the morning, science will be fresh,
because each day starts anew,
and (it is written) He wants us to be happy,
      so we are.

God recreates us in His image
every day—little mystery martians
      sans spare rib

to make her
to make us happy,

even though we are not whole
and never will be.

There is no need to study; as always,
the answers will reveal themselves
      to be
as simple as a sunset.

Indiana Memories

Indiana pizzeria finds itself at the center of 'religious freedom' debate.   *–Ed Payne, CNN, April 3, 2015*

Jesus would not refuse
to serve a stranger pizza.
He would
make the stranger an extra-large,
stuffed-crust pizza,
hand-tossed
with all the toppings
and extra cheese.
He would
sit the stranger in a vinyl booth
right up front
by the pane-glass window,
and wash the stranger's feet.
He would
invite His twelve best friends
to dine
with the stranger,
     and
He would
make them pizza too.
He would
take five anchovy pizzas
and two orders of bread sticks
to the patio
and feed five thousand
diverse attendees
at a gay wedding.
He would
do unto others
as He would have them
do unto Him . . .
and turn water
into wine,
because that is what He does
at weddings.

Today's Poem

It is completely free of rhetoric
and states only the facts.

As I suspect you can tell,
the tone is dry (like my inkwell)

and it shows no emotion
(like my mirror).

But it is written
in more or less good grammar

and properly punctuated.
Perhaps, that is all one can ask

of a muse too busy
drafting a Petition for Review

to the Texas Supreme Court
to trifle in verse.

ii.

Small Things

It is always the small things,
the contours,

the way her rag-doll hair
fits tightly into a bun
and exposes her neck. The way
she stands on her toes, and
how she acts first
without saying a word
then smiles.

The way her tattered jeans
cover her Doc Martins, and the way
she holds her beer bottle
like a teacup.

Her kisses are always gentle,
her cheeks dew-kissed
and pink.

The way she doesn't wear a bra
or need to, and the way she doesn't care
when I notice.

How her nose crinkles
when she's silly. The way she cries
without tears.

The way she walks away
on the tips of her toes
without a word.

The Little Nun That Could
for Jill

When lift plus thrust is greater than
load plus drag, anything can fly.

There is a moment when
the wind drifts at just the right
angle, rustling leaves, teasing
my habit. I have just the right
song in my heart, producing
lift. The aerodynamics of the
soul is unknown; it's the purity
of my body, the naivety of my
mind. Nothing tells me I can
not fly, so I try.

My Would-Be Wife

The wife of my dreams would be
making pancakes for her nine-year-old son

early on Saturday morning
while listening to the Beatles' *Abby Road*,
                almost dancing,
whisking the mix
until the pan casts heat.

My would-be wife would be
playing Ludwig van Beethoven's 32 sonatas
on piano, some Johannes Brahms
and Sergei Rachmaninoff.
If she truly loves me, she would play
Wolfgang Mozart too.

My wife would run
another Air Force half-marathon
with me and our dog, Celeste,
                putting respective baggage
behind us—our loves and our losses—
our childhoods behind us.

I want a wife who would
appreciates the small things: taking trash out,
walking the dog(s), driving the boy
to guitar lessons, to his father's house,
to school,
to his gigs, the park.

My would-be wife would
be more than delighted
                with a one-room cabin
that I build in the boonies with bare hands,
no Starbucks for decades and the Wi-Fi
won't work.

My would-be wife would be
reading this stupid poem and laughing,
because she would simply want to be
my wife.

Ars Domestica

I should be making pesto,
because you will be home soon,
and you will want to get started.

I have been alone
in the house (for a change),
and all I have done

is wash the morning dishes,
sweep the floor,
and do laundry.

I took all three dogs for a walk,
one at a time,
because . . .

well, you know.

I managed to shower and shave,
and I changed the bed sheets.
Now, I am writing a poem.

I hate this feeling—

as if I've done something wrong.
I did not make the milk jugs leak.
It's not my fault the dogs
rolled in the morning dew and
brought the dampness in.
I did not know you were
saving the pickles for Max.
Your taxes are due, and
you used your last check last night.
(I thought you were happy
you could now change your name.)
It's not my fault you're a woman.
I did not design your body.
I'm sorry you don't have time
to practice, to run with Celeste,
to spend time with your son,
to sleep late, to be alone.
I was only trying to help.

The Rain Begins

It almost smells like autumn.
Your bags are packed
and stacked neatly by the bedroom door.

I know you don't like chaos,
so I dress quietly in the dark

and leave for work early.
I make a mental note:
get a winter coat before coming home.

The rain begins,
as I catch the train to the city.

The Honeymoon That Was Not

The sound is heartbreaking. It is
the echoes after a slamming door,
after the engine guns and the sobs.

Traces of teardrops on burning
cheek are paths from bloodshot eyes
to a sea of wasted intentions.

That memory is a hazardous haze
seething in her soul, moments before.
The sun rises, and you realize

you dodged a searing slug of lead.
She had not yet filled your sock drawer
with her panties and bras.

All she abandoned was a blue sweater,
the one she never did like at all,
a gift from her mother—

the woman who left her father,
herself and her sisters, who had bailed
while the girls dressed like whores

for their prom. Those were
her memories and was what she did.
That night, she in turn left her fiancé

(the only man she had loved
since childhood) and decided to marry
only someone she could despise,

which meant she would never
marry anyone, because she never
learned to hate anyone save her mother,

who had slammed that screen door
and squealed that Trans Am's tires,
and who never said goodbye.

Missing Pieces

I ordered replacement parts
for my heart on craigslist. The maker
gave guarantees—

special delivery, satisfaction.
My first impression upon receiving the package
was that the box is empty.

Of course, the instruction pages
in three languages make it perfectly clear:
Love is not included.

This is a starter kit;
it fits the dimensions well enough
but must be filled with time.

Winter Storm

I was watching the geese
fly outside my window, not searching
the internet for my past.

Your face appeared
out of history, and my thoughts
flooded the superhighway.

I was stranded
in a vortex of yesterday's mistakes—
out of gas, tires flat.

iii.

The Meeting Ran Long

Let me begin again. The day was cooler than I thought, and the meeting ran long. Afterward, I sat alone in the room at the conference table to reflect on life. I pretended I was a wealthy nobleman and the half-empty coffee cups and saucers were my subjects. The two dented coke cans where Deborah sat were the only servants in the room. I gloated in my gluttony.

I could have waved my hand, dismissing both subjects and servants, but I wanted to make an example of someone. I ordered the coke cans to bring me a saucer, but neither can moved. I raised my voice again, pounding the table. The cans revolted. The cups and saucers rallied around them. I was outnumbered, the only man in the room. I cursed my misfortune.

I give myself permission

Yesterday, I rode the roller coaster
of my manic depression
          at an amusement park
that was somewhat less than amusing.
I wanted to drink in the afternoon,
but I knew if I did, I could not run
with my dog in the evening,
as has become our custom.

Today, my knees hurt,
clear evidence of my age.
I give myself permission to open a beer before noon
(as if time matters).
          And I sip it, knowing I will be
falling down before evening,
then Buster will drag me
through the park as I stumble.

Tomorrow, my brain will bleed.
I will be happy that the pain is only temporary,
until the next day when the carnival will beckon
and the tilt-a-whirl will suck my soul
into its blender, and I will puke
on my new shoes, and I
will lie on the ground
unable to crawl.

Not a Squirrel

"What do you mean?" the hedgehog said. "Can't you see I'm not a squirrel?"

Honestly, I had to look closer. I mean, he really did look like a squirrel, except his tail was short, and his face . . . yeah, his face looked all scrunched up and kind of mousy. He could easily have been a porcupine, because his fur didn't look soft at all. It's not like I'd seen a lot of porcupines, but I'd heard stories.

On second thought, he wasn't nearly as cute as most squirrels I'd seen. Of course, I wasn't going to tell the critter that. He seemed a little ill-tempered and not very friendly at all. I wondered whether he might be a badger or a wolverine. They say those things can be vicious and nasty, and I didn't want to find out for myself.

"I guess you're right." I offered by way of apology. "My bad."

He continued to glare at me, and I wondered again about the badger. I mean, I really didn't want to know how nasty this rodent could be. I wasn't even sure whether whatever he was was in the rodent family. Did he have rodent brothers or sisters? How about rodent cousins?

I could stand it no longer, but I had to be delicate—use tact and finesse. I wasn't looking to hurt any feelings. And I didn't want to get my face torn off. I especially didn't want that.

"So . . ." I started slowly and began to back away. "Are you a badger?"

Not Quite Empty

Eric Blanchard is an empty parking lot—
only not quite empty. He has
one beat-up Oldsmobile parked
under his lamp light.
The head lamps of the Oldsmobile
are broken. Two teenage boys
held batting practice on its windshield.
Eric has faded lines
dividing his parking spaces
and a pothole with standing water
in the middle of spot 5A.
The Oldsmobile has a flat tire.
It has bird shit on its canvas top.
The lamp light only lights half the lot.

Kicking and Screaming

It's always a mad dash,
at the absolute last minute.

But, with your flip-flopped foot
a brick and a half down

on the pedal, you make it there
in record time, again,

driving with the focus of a mother
whose cub is going to be late

for his cello lesson. He is
strapped in the back seat, kicking

and screaming, because he
really wants to be at the park

with his friends, and he
wanted to play the guitar.

Something Else Domestic

I cannot shake the feeling
I should be doing laundry
or washing dishes or something
       else domestic
to make things easier
for everyone. Maxwell
is wearing the same pair of black pants
he wore yesterday
and the day before that.
       Of course,
that's the way he likes it. He
would never wear the blue jeans
that have been clean
and hanging in the basement
for two or three weeks
even if his life depended on it.
I guess it's a good thing
that his life doesn't.

Head-Cold Apocalypse

Like a zombie,
having swallowed a Benadryl
to keep my head from exploding,
I keep wishing

it was cyanide, so the warm blood
of the living would not lure me,
club-foot after club-foot,
toward the people I still love,

the people I hunger for,
wanting/not wanting,
to inflict this stale-brained life/death
upon the almost innocent

(or the not-so innocent)
        living—
the tragic and not-so tragic
victims of my undead affliction,
this walking pneumonia.

Cigarette-Smoke Nostalgia

Who knew?   A whiff
could conjure up memories—
wafting like teenage rebellion.

So unwelcome
in the aged conformity of this
day-in, day-out, every day
life,

no time for ill-advised tendencies,
bad habits, desk job.

Cool high school pride
hanging outside gymnasium lockers,

leaning against
strategic door jambs.

Post-pubescent angst
impregnates full-frontal cortex,
consuming lingering gray cells
like cancer.

Recreational Use

If I come to Oregon to see you
and rent a one-bedroom, shit-hole apartment
furnished with a used kitchen table,
a folding chair,
and a queen-size Coleman air mattress
        with built-in air pump
I inflate in the corner at night,

would you believe
that it is fate,
that we are meant to be together,
and that I am the one?

Or would you suspect for a second
that I am actually here
to put together pieces
à la blank slate
in the Pacific Northwest,

where I have always wanted to live
in the wild
        and where
recreational use is legal?

Eric Blanchard was born and raised in Houston, Texas. In college, Eric studied a variety of subjects, including theater, journalism, psychology, and English, eventually earning degrees in philosophy (B.A.) and jurisprudence (J.D.). After practicing law for a decade and a half, Eric moved to Ohio, where he wrote and taught for several years; whence, he returned home to help care for his parents. During his legal career, Eric argued cases in appellate courts, acted as editor-in-chief of an international trade law journal, and worked as an adviser for a representative in the Texas legislature.

Eric's poetry has been published in a variety of journals and reviews, both online and in hard copy, including *Hanging Moss Journal, Autumn Sky Poetry, Wilderness House Literary Review, Rust + Moth, Oak Bend Review, Breadcrumb Scabs, Borderlands: Texas Poetry Review, Pudding Magazine, Vending Machine: Poetry for Change, Mock Turtle Zine, Common Threads 2012, Amarillo Bay, Literary Orphans, Turbulence Poetry, Poetry Quarterly, The Rusty Nail Magazine, Vector Press, Light,* and *Shot Glass Journal.* In 2013, his prose poem "The Meeting Ran Long" was nominated for Sundress Publications' "Best of the Net" anthology.

Eric has been active in numerous poetry organizations and workshops. He was a charter member of the Wright Library Poets in Dayton, Ohio and is a member of the Ohio Poetry Association. He is also a member of the Poetry Society of Texas and Poets Northwest in Houston.

www.ingramcontent.com/pod-product-compliance
Lightning Source LLC
LaVergne TN
LVHW051612080426
835510LV00020B/3262